INTERNATIONAL OUT-OF-PLACE ARTIFACTS EXPERT

KLAUS DONA

Digging for Answers...
and Finding More Questions

LAUREL STEINHICE

The LightSource Group

lightsourcegroup.com

D1706531

ISBN: 978-0-9830003-0-3

Photos provided by Klaus Dona from his personal archives, and used by permission.

Photos and captions of the artifacts pictured in this book are drawn from the exhibit catalog of the "Unexplained Mysteries" Exhibit, "Die Welt des Unerklaerlichen", which appeared at the Vienna Art Center Schottenstift, Wien, in 2001.

Cover design, text layout, graphic elements and production provided by Thom W. King, KingAuthor Creative, P.O. Box 50214, Nashville, TN 37205

Printed in the United States of America.

For more information or bulk book orders visit:
www.lightsourcegroup.com

The LightSource Group

lightsourcegroup.com

TABLE OF CONTENTS

ACKNOWLEGEMENTS

I note with great appreciation the photographic skills and professional publishing expertise of Thom King of KingAuthor Creative, and wish to also thank my good friend Alletta Bell who has shared so many journeys of discovery with me – including this one!

I am indebted to my children Chris and Eileen, for their patience and support, and for the joy I've had in our sharing a lifelong interest in history, pre-history, and in the great mysteries of this fascinating planet on which we live.

Photos are provided by Klaus Dona. Photos and captions of the artifacts pictured in this book are drawn from the exhibit catalog of the "Unexplained Mysteries" Exhibit, "Die Welt des Unerklaerlichen", which appeared at the Vienna Art Center Schottenstift, Wien, in 2001.

Most of all, my thanks go to Klaus Dona, who lives the adventure ... and lets me write about it!

Laurel Steinhice, 2011

Klaus and Laurel

DEDICATION

To all the seekers of Truth and Light, everywhere. May you share the great awakenings of these special times in which we live.

We are both dwarfed by infinity, and embraced by it. As we shift our focus to the very beginnings of life of Earth, there is a timelessness about it.

We are here ... we are now ... and we are a part of all that has gone before.

There is so much to share!

FOREWORD

I'd never been to Hawaii before, and the endless vistas of sea and sky kept pulling my attention away from the January 2010 Earth Transformation Conference I had come there to attend. Crashing waves pounding against the rocky shoreline dusted me lightly with salt spray and would have lulled me to sleep in a hotel deck chair, if I let them – but the conference had much to offer, too, and I didn't want to miss the next speaker's presentation on Out of Place Artifacts.

I've always been interested in the early history of the planet. I read Ignatius Donnelly's "Atlantis, the Antediluvian World" (first published in 1884) decades ago, and latched onto Erich von Daniken's "Chariots of the Gods" when it first came out in 1966. More recently, I've been challenged to keep up with the steady stream of books and documentaries about amazing archaeological discoveries that seem to point to a legacy of pre-history far older and far more complex than we had even begun to guess at.

Since the subject was already of strong interest to me, I looked forward to hearing what the speaker, Klaus Dona, had to say. After having acknowledged a disaffection for public speaking (he would have preferred to be in the jungle on a "dig") and the discomfort he felt at having his luggage lost in transit (a situation all too many fellow-travelers could relate to!), he jumped right into the OOPARTS material headfirst.

His style was simple, direct and authoritative. He obviously knew his stuff! Beyond that, his own enthusiasm for the subject matter came through loud and clear. When it came to Out of Place Artifacts, the man was in his element.

Within the first three minutes he had captured my attention. At the end of his two-hour presentation I was left wanting more, and hoping that I might meet him.

I saw my chance the next day, dusted off my second-language skills, and greeted him in German.. (He is Austrian.) I was hoping that the novelty of that approach would get me past the group of others who wanted his attention, and it worked. We connected, found several points of common interest, and soon I had that wonderful feeling of having found a long-lost friend.

We kept in touch after the conference ended, and six months later I showed up on his Vienna doorstep to interview him for the book he had graciously consented to let me write about him – this one!

It has been a joy and delight to write! I hope our readers enjoy it.

Laurel Steinhice,
Nashville, Tennessee, USA, 2011

WHO IS KLAUS DONA?

Klaus Dona is a multifaceted person who can't be summed up into a single definitive phrase. There is a simple open charm about him that puts one at ease and inspires trust, yet a closer look reveals a deeply complex individual who leads a delightfully adventurous life.

He's a hard man to keep up with! If you walk beside him, you'll be challenged to match his brisk pace. He strides forth with clear purpose and boundless energy, whether on the streets and byways of Vienna or along life's pathway toward thrilling new discoveries.

Metaphysically-minded people gravitate toward Klaus and are quick to see that there's something special about him. Yet he makes no claims. If there is a reliance on unseen powers or gifts in his repertoire, it is entirely instinctive and largely unrecognized. Whatever magic he has is neatly tucked away in his back pocket, not to be put on display for 'show and tell'. He readily acknowledges that unusual things just seem to happen to him out of the blue, but if you ask him why, he simply says "I don't know."

There are those who see the presence of a powerful shaman in him, but when someone mentions the idea it always takes him by surprise. He gets that "Who, *me*?" look on his face. It's not that he's in denial. He seems quite open to possibilities. It's just that he refuses to lay official claim to something he can't actually *prove,* and won't accept even a speculative scenario unless it has a certain weight of logic behind it.

Klaus has managed to maintain a healthy skepticism without buying into society's long dogmatic list of rigid 'impossibilities'. This approach serves him well in the present focus of his work, which is centered on bringing OOPARTS (Out of Place Artifacts) to light toward a broader understanding of Earth's long, diverse cultural history.

An inquiring mind is just the first step for him. The inner drive to find, to understand, to *know,* will not be satisfied by mere speculation. He takes the analytical approach, in which every significant artifact must be submitted to a network of experts for rigorous scientific examination. Where there are fakes and frauds, they must be exposed and discredited. Where there is authenticity, it must be clearly understood and further investigated, to the highest possible degree.

How far will it go? Will Klaus Dona's explorations, along with those of others like him, lead us to a much broader paradigm of understanding the history of our planet?

That remains to be seen.

We can see that he's on the track of that goal, though – and we can feel, instinctively, that he's the right man for the job.

The Force is with him.

CHAPTER 1

THE CRYSTAL WATERS

*Klaus with his friend Padre Huertas
in Colombia, examining an artifact.*

When you go looking for giants' bones in the Andes Mountains, you never know what you might find.

Klaus Dona is quick to tell you he's not an archaeologist, per se – he's a researcher, and an exhibit curator and director. His present focus is on seeking out mysterious artifacts (OOPARTS) to be carefully examined, authenticated, dated and documented, after which selected items are presented to the public in a series of exhibitions and lectures.

He digs for answers in the Andes and all over the globe, not only in the earth itself, but also in the storeroom shelves of private collectors who have invited him to see – and to photograph – the remarkable items in their collections. And when he's in the company of local folk, whether under a shade tree on a rocky hillside, having coffee in a sidewalk cafe or conferring in a carefully protected storage room full of artifacts, the conversation is sure to turn to other finds, other "digs", other collections, and other wonders in the region.

"In the year 2000 I came first to Quito, " Klaus recalls, "and I was introduced by an Austrian Dr. and shaman, Dr. Valentin Hampejs to the collection of German Villamar (the pyramid with the eye and other 350 artifacts). In 2001 on my second trip to South America I drove with German Villamar to La Mana, where I was introduced to Ing Guillermo Sotomayor, who had found those artifacts 1984 while golddigging."

"He is also the one who found many of the significant artifacts, as well as the water I am going to tell you about," Dona continues. "In 2004 on a trip with a water-specialist from Austria, I had two days time and we drove down to the south to Loja, were I could find the family of padre Vaca, who found the giant bones in 1964."

Klaus had done his homework.and was on the track of specific items his research had focused on. But that was just the beginning! Having already located and photographed the giants bones he was looking for, he turned his attention to the waters of a special spring in the area, that were said to have curative powers.

The water was pure and sweet, with a degree of absolute clarity that is seldom seen these days. He was intrigued, and asked for some samples to take back to Europe with him for further study. His companions filled ten 1½ liter bottles, and packed them in a sturdy carton he could take with him. For the long flight home, he checked the box through to destination, along with his suitcase.

But it wasn't going to be that easy.

As he sat in the Guayaquil airport awaiting his flight, an official-looking fellow approached him and asked "did you check through a cardboard box?"

"Yes," Klaus readily agreed.

"You must come with me," he was informed.

He was taken to a small room where he saw his cardboard box sitting on a table ... under the watchful eyes of fifteen armed policemen, holding rifles.

"Sit down." A chair was provided for him, and the questions began.

"Is this your box?"

"Yes", Klaus verified that it was indeed his.

"What's in it?"

"Bottles of spring water, " he clarified.

At this point, Klaus's heart sank and unpleasant thoughts began running through his mind. *Could someone have put drugs in the box with the water? Is that what the officials are looking for? Man, I could be in really deep trouble, here!*

He watched, sweating nervously, as they put the box – *his* box – on the belt, and ran it through a security scanner.

He watched. They did the same again and again.. Then they brought it to the table in front of him, and said "Open it and unpack it."

He did, and saw to his great relief that there were. indeed, his bottles of water inside ... and nothing else. No plastic bags of white powder that might be cocaine, as he had feared.

"What's in the bottles?" they asked him.

"Water." He gave them the same answer as before.

They ran the bottles through the scanner again.

"And why do you want to take it out of this country with you?" They continued their inquiry.

"I was told the water from this spring is very pure and special," he answered honestly, "and I wanted to take some with me to have it tested."

"Hmmph!" The inquisitor sniffed derisively, as if that were a ridiculous idea.

For half an hour or so nothing more was said, and Klaus just sat there looking at the guns pointed in his direction.

They had sent for a doctor.

He got there and opened his medical bag, produced a hypodermic needle and stuck it through one of the plastic bottles, to draw out a sample of the water.

Again, Klaus's heart sank. Could they have put something illegal directly into the water? They, *who?* He couldn't think of anyone he had offended, who might want to set him up for this kind of trouble. Again, he was sweating.

The doctor took his water sample and left; after another nervous wait, the investigator came back and let him know the inquiry was over.

"You can go."

Klaus breathed a sigh of relief – and he wanted a cigarette!

"Is there anywhere I could go to have a cigarette?" he asked.

"NO SMOKING!" the official bellowed at him, angrily.

"Ok, ok, I don't smoke..." Klaus didn't argue, as he beat a quick retreat out of the presence of those armed guards.

At every stopover after that on the long journey home, Klaus held his breath. He halfway expected to be called to be questioned about his box full of water, again.

It happened, but (mercifully!) not until he was going through customs at his home destination, Vienna.

They ran his box through the scanner ... paused ... ran it through again, and yet again. "What have you got in there?" they asked him.

"Water from a spring in Ecuador," he explained yet again. "It's supposed to be a very special water, very pure, and I brought some back to have it tested..."

He began to explain, about the 2001 OOPARTS Exhibit in Vienna, "Unsolved Mysteries", and that he was still collecting material for further exhibits.

"I went to that exhibit twice!" one of the customs officials spoke up.

That was a big help! They talked about the exhibit for a few minutes, and the official said he and his family had enjoyed it very much.

"Do you know why they asked you about the box?" the customs officer asked, after it had been opened, inspected, cleared and released.

"I have no idea!" Klaus admitted.

"Come here and I'll show you ..." He took Klaus to a position behind the scanner where Klaus could see the screen, and ran the box through once more"

There was nothing on the screen. No water; no bottles; no box. Nothing. The energy of the water was so strong, it interfered with the scanner's ability to read an image. When tested later by experts, the water registered a higher energy content than any previously tested water had shown; several times higher than the healing waters of Fatima.[1]

---

[1] The water at Fatima had been tested at 640,000 Bovi. Klaus's water samples from Ecuador tested at 1.5 million Bovi, and when it was re-tested 6 years later it had not lost the power of its natural energy.

"Did you find anything else interesting on this trip?" the official asked conversationally, as Klaus gathered his luggage and prepared to depart.

"Why yes I did," Klaus replied, and added confidentially, "I have some bones of a 7.6 meter giant in my suitcase ..."

They shared a hearty laugh, and Klaus went on his way with his box of water ... and his suitcase, in which some bones of an ultra-ancient 7.6 meter giant were neatly packed in with his clothes.

.

CHAPTER 2

ON THE TRAIL OF
THE LOST RECORDS

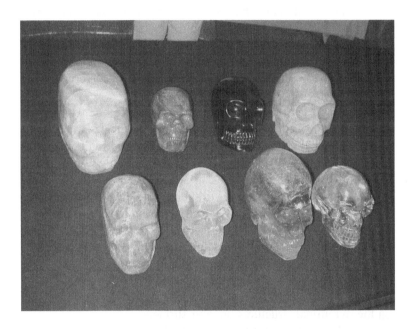

Here are a set of crystal skulls that have been exhibited as part of Klaus Dona's "Unsolved Mysteries" collection. How were they made? By whom? What do they mean? We don't know

The late great seer Edgar Cayce (1877 – 1945) often spoke of the "...lost records of Atlantis", and prophesied that examples of these forgotten archives would be found in our times. Among those most commonly mentioned are one cache in the paw of the Great Sphinx, another in its shoulder, and an important remnant of Atlantean civilization off Bimini, near an undersea freshwater spring.

Cayce has led us to expect that they will come to light in our lifetimes! It's exciting to think it can happen ... but even when we want to believe it, most people have nagging doubts. Will it really happen? Or as it a pipedream?

Once again, we're in the realm of unanswered questions. If a set of "lost records" *is* found, how would we know it's the real thing?

What would it look like?

Different people have different ideas on that. Some say tablets of gold, incised with strange symbols that have to be decoded. Some say there is a vast hall of records that lies buried in the sand not far from the pyramids of Gizeh.[2] – along with additional pyramids that are also scheduled for discovery any day now.

Some say there may be the remnants of stone temples – and even stone cities! – still standing, beneath the ocean depths.

Others look to cuneiform and pre-cuneiform clay tablets from Sumeria and Akkadia[3] for retrieval of forgotten information ... and of course there are the Dead Sea Scrolls found in the caves of Qumran in 1947. They are still being studied and translated. We don't think of them as Atlantean, but they would certainly qualify as "lost records".

Some say crystal skulls hold the data of the lost records electronically, as our modern computer chips can hold vast collections of data – and that the same may be true for other crystals, especially those that are called "record keepers" based on the pyramidal structures on their surfaces.

Why not all of those, and more?

---

[2] The Antiquities Minister of Egypt vehemently denies that such a hall of records ever existed, and refuses permission to allow an archaeological dig on the site where it is thought to be.
[3] Zecheriah Sitchen has done highly-detailed research on these and other Middle-Eastern artifacts.

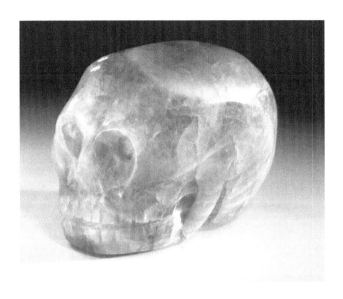

This particular crystal skull is made of rose quartz.

Our concept of "lost records", per se, is broadening. Rather than a single form of data recording, we are beginning to understand that there are many. And rather than a single source or location, we are discovering wonders and mysteries in all the nooks and crannies of our world.

Advances in science and technology offer the modern seeker of ultra-ancient information new opportunities not only for finding the artifacts, but also for evaluating and deciphering them. Klaus Dona and others like him have more tools now than ever before, in discovering, identifying and assembling the pieces of the great puzzle of life on Earth.

The great mysteries must still be considered to be unsolved – yet with every pertinent artifact or resource that comes to light, the broad outlines of those puzzles come more clearly into focus.

Klaus on expedition in the Andes, with his friend and guide.

Interest in OOPARTS and the whole range of related topics is high these days, and shows no sign of having peaked. When his interviews for The Camelot project were posted on YouTube in the Spring of 2010, they drew over 80,000 hits in the first few days.

There are new television documentaries, DVDs and books coming out every day, and Klaus's quest for (more!) answers is by no means over.

He has put out the call for those who have something to share with him, inviting them to contact him – and the calls are coming in! A lot of people seem to want to join him (at least in spirit!), as he digs for more answers – even though it so often means finding more questions.

Klaus shows off some treasured artifacts on a foggy day, with the Andes Mountains in the background. Note the skull cradled in the crook of his left arm. Where are these priceless antiquities now? In the keeping of their rightful owners, usually in the countries of origin in which they were found.

Klaus and his guide take time out for a quick photo pose, before returning to their dig.

*Klaus is dwarfed by the gigantic ancient monument beside him,
set on a flat-topped jungle pyramid in Tula, Mexico.*

CHAPTER 3

THE TIMES OF HIS LIFE

*Here is Klaus as a toddler, beginning to
explore the wilds of his native Austrian Tirol..*

Klaus Dona was born in 1949 in the Austrian Tyrol, at a
time of economic and political uncertainty. The Zeitgeist[4] was a
scrambled mixture of hopes and fears, just on the edge of
grounding into what would come to be called the "Cold War" era.
A generation and a half ago, the great "war to

---

[4] spirit of the times

end all wars"[5] had failed to live up to its press releases. Its destructive path across Europe had been followed by a peace treaty so haphazard and unjust as to be regarded by many historians, now, as "the peace to end all peace". The Austro-Hungarian Empire, with the surviving members of its longstanding historical Habsburg monarchy deposed and forced into exile, lay on the 1919 conference table before the victorious Allies, to be carved up like a Christmas goose.

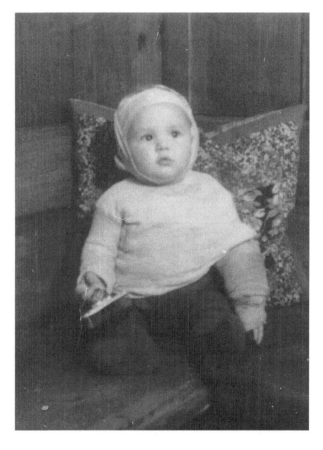

Even as a tiny fellow, Klaus had a thoughtful look!

---

[5] World War I

Various bits and pieces of the Imperial holdings were parceled out to their nearest neighboring victor-nations as spoils of war, but the sociopolitical architects of a new Europe didn't stop there. Hungary was granted the stand-alone independence it sought, but that still wasn't the end of it. The map-makers seemed to have a penchant for creating new nations, right and left.

Young Klaus, sharing a moment of his happy childhood with his mother.

The assorted ethnic constituencies[6] that suddenly found themselves with flags and parliaments of their own had been demanding independence – but they had no real experience of it. And self-government wasn't an easy thing to manage on the basis of on-the-job training. Even Austria itself, the remnant centerpoint of a bygone global Empire, had a hard time getting its parliamentary republican act together. And then before you knew it, here came a Second World War on the heels of the first.

Austria was annexed and occupied by neighboring Nazi Germany, and steamrollered into a crushing, brutal conflict. At the end of the war, it was occupied again by the victorious Allies – even though it had been officially categorized as a liberated

---

[6] among them Czechoslovakia and Bosnia-Herzegovina

nation, rather than a belligerent one.[7] Vienna was declared a quadripartite city, like its fellow Germanic capital Berlin, to the North, and contingents of the British, American, French and Soviet Armed Forces took over a joint responsibility for running the city – and their respective Zones of the Austrian nation.

Klaus was a child who loved animals and zoos.

By the time Klaus arrived on the scene as an infant, the Allied occupation had been in place for about four and a half years ... but things had already turned sour between the Soviets and the Western Allies. The Berlin Blockade was clear evidence of Stalin's agenda toward driving the Western powers out of Europe. How far could he push them, without risking an all-out

---

[7] This was partly in recognition that the Austrians – and especially those of the Tyrolean province – had stepped into the fight against Hitler during the latter part of the war, and had at least partially succeeded in self-liberation. They greeted the American Armies warmly, when the troops marched into Innsbruck.

new war? If Berlin fell, was West Germany next? And what about Austria?

Czechoslovakia had already slipped into the heavy folds of the Iron Curtain, along with Poland, Yugoslavia, Romania, Albania, Bulgaria and the Baltic states of Latvia, Estonia and Lithuania. Hungary would not be far behind.[8] And there sat Austria in the middle of it all, at the crossroads between East and West ... as usual.

Germany was in the process of being split into East Germany and West Germany, a division that would last until reunification came at last, in 1989. Would Austria suffer a similar fate?

And if not, would Austria be an Eastern Bloc nation, or a Western Bloc nation? Or would it somehow manage to stand above the fray as a neutral nation, like Switzerland? Young Klaus knew nothing of such matters in his early childhood, which was spent in a quiet village nestled in the Tyrolean Alps. Just beyond his doorstep stood the kind of scenery that makes one think of Julie Andrews and "The Sound of Music".

As the political tug-of-war over his homeland went on, he learned to walk and talk in the household of his widowed mother and his two siblings. And by the time he was a schoolboy of six, the last Allied soldier of occupation was on the way out of his country.[9]

Austria, like Klaus, had a lot to learn! There would be challenges along the way, of course. But for the boy and his nation alike, it was a time of unprecedented freedom and opportunity, in which to chart one's own course in life. And they would make the most of it.

---

[8] Hungary fell to the Soviet-backed communists in 1956.
[9] Oct. 25, 1955

CHAPTER 4

OF MONUMENTS AND MYTHS

*Many South and Central American pyramids take the familiar
flat-topped form, and feature steps by which one
may climb to the top.*

Almost as soon as he learned to read, young Klaus Dona took an interest in the cultures and history of the Earth. He was fascinated by monuments, myths and mysteries – and especially the pyramids.

Who built them?

When were they built, and *how?*

What were they intended to be? Tombs for the ancient kings of Egypt? Or more than that?

The Eqyptian pyramids, such as these, are visible from Space. Were they intended as (among other things!) landmarks and navigational aids for space travelers? It seems a logical possibility, but it can't be proven.

As he grew to manhood, his interest in the pyramids stayed with him – and still plays a role in his life today.

"Pyramids are a symbol form for wisdom and knowledge," Klaus notes in the text of a catalog for his "Unsolved Mysteries" Exhibit, which features a broad selection of Out of Place Artifacts.[10] And further, "...the order of the stars

---

[10] The exhibit has been shown (to date) in Vienna, Berlin, Interlaken, and Seoul.

of the Orion Belt exactly match with the pattern of the pyramids of Gizeh".

Surely that cannot be an accident. What did the ancients know about the constellations in the heavens above them?

He goes on to note that pyramids exist not only in Egypt but also in China, Mongolia, South and Central America, and even in Greece, France, and the Canary Islands. There is a small pyramid in Austria, and a larger one has been recently discovered (and has yet to be fully unearthed and studied) in Bosnia.

"There were found in Bosnia two pyramids, bigger than the great pyramid in Egypt.". he reports. "An old and destroyed pyramid was just found in Sardinia. Another pyramid was found in Peru, and Bolivian archaeologists reported about a pyramid under the earth with its top approximately 10 meters under ground. So far, we can only speculate as to how old must this pyramid be."

Dona is among those who feel that the pyramids are, on the whole, much older than the age-ranges that are commonly assigned to them.

Nor are the disagreements between various experts on the *age* of the pyramids, per se.

The pyramid of the shining eye[11], found in Ecuador, is small enough to be held in the hand. It has 13 steps and a capstone featuring an eye, and looks a lot like the image on the U.S. $1.00 bill. When shown in black light, it reveals a powerful radiance. Inlaid in gold on its base is a depiction of the Orion constellation, along with some incised notations in an unknown writing.

Found in the same cache with the pyramid are a stone incised with the precise illustration of how the pyramid is to be hand-held, and another showing a helmeted figure holding the pyramid as wavy lines (suggesting energy-rays) flow from it toward two lesser figures. The helmet on the illustration shows what appears to be an antenna protruding from its crown.

No antennae have been found, as yet, but a bowl-shaped helmet was found beside the other items, and bears a hole in its center into which an antenna might have been attached.

---

[11]Shown on the cover photo.

Shining pyramid with "divine eye". This pyramid stone is the most important artifact among the strange relics found in Ecuador in the 1980s. It was been the model for many pyramids pictured on various stones. On the stone are engraved 13 steps and fluorescing elements that shine under the influence of ultraviolet light. A dozen other artifacts from La Mana show the same effects.

According to rumor, there should exist three original pyramid stones in the world. One relic is said to be in the Rothschild family collections, and another is said to be in the "Witch Museum" in Brussels.The third was long said to be in Ecuador.

No definitive translation of the writing on the pyramid's base has been determined, but a noted language expert, Prof. Kurt Schildmann, the former president of the German Linguistic society,   classified the inscriptions as being a part of a language older than any he had ever seen. His best guess at a translation was "the son of the creator comes".

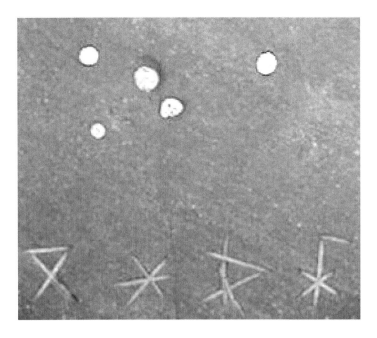

When one lifts the Shining "divine eye" pyramid and looks at the bottom of the stone, there is yet another interesting mystery. Some points are marked that correspond with the Orion constellation. There are also some script-like symbols, which have been translated as "from there comes the son of the creator", by a linguist. What does it all mean? We don't know.

Yet the deeper meanings of the pyramids, large and small, are coming forward for a new level of consideration as explorers and researchers step beyond the idea that they are no more than tombs, per se, and now begin to regard them as 'temples, holy places, symbols of the world, and sources of mysterious forces'.

When he was a lad, young Dona had no way of knowing that he would someday be among those 'explorers and researchers' who pondered the mysteries of the pyramids ... but they drew him, even then. Having decided that he wanted to be a cook, he studied for a profession of "hotelier" – but in his mind's eye he was cooking up something more adventurous than schnitzel and potato salad!

Our world is so full of mysteries! They tugged at his attention, and led him to a reading list that included books like Ignatious Donnelly's "Atlantis: The Antediluvian World" (1884) and Thomas Sugrue's "There is a River", an account of the life and work of Edgar Cayce. By the time Erich von Daniken's "Chariots of the Gods" came out (in 1966) he was already prepared to be fascinated by it – and marveled over pictures of the Nazca lines and the map of Piri Reis.

Every exposure to the legacies of the past caught his attention and inspired him to wonder. How old *is* this planet, anyway? Who were the first to be called "men", to walk upon it? And what connection might there be between ancient myths of gods and goddesses and the history of the humanity?

When Plato wrote about Atlantis, was it just an entertaining tale, or an allegory of an ideal society? Or was there something solid and historical behind it?

Why are there so *many* stories worldwide, about Atlantis and Lemuria; about a land of Mu and great civilizations that have been destroyed by cataclysms. What wondrous cities may there have been, that lived and died and sank beneath the sea?

Is there a seed of truth in these stories?

And if so, how do we tell the difference between that true seed and the made-up embellishments that have been added, to decorate it? That's the really important part. Idle speculation was never enough for Klaus. He kept looking for the truth behind the myth.

A broad understanding of the Earth is like a giant puzzle. As he found more fragmentary pieces of early history, he kept trying to fit them together.

He kept reading.

He kept looking for answers.

And instead, he kept finding more questions.

Examples of pyramids from all over the world.
The form is a widespread ancient architectural theme.

CHAPTER 5

MARCHING FROM ONE ERA INTO ANOTHER

*Klaus (at left) with his Army buddies,
in front of their tank.*

When Klaus had completed his formal education, military service was next. That was educational, to! It helped to deepen his understandings and broaden his horizons.

It's probably fair to say that the regimented world of barracks, mess halls, parade grounds, all-day full-pack hikes and maneuvers didn't come naturally to an independent fellow like Klaus. But he was adaptable, and it was a good thing to have a working knowledge of that environment, along with the skills it had to teach. And again, there were both *timely* and *timeless* elements in the experience.

On an immediate basis, the international political climate was still highly uncertain.

"They called it the 'Praha[12] Spring'," he recalls. "Because the Austrian government had helped Czech refugees, we were thinking there would be a war between Austria and Soviet Russia. My comrades and I were ready to fight for our country. It was a serious situation in1968."

"Every Austrian man from the age of 18 has to enter to the army," he recalls, "but I didn't wait to be drafted."

Klaus with members of his Austrian Army unit.
He's the one standing, at the far right.

Klaus already knew that he wanted to see the world, and had tasted a bit of travel .

"When I returned from Paris," he remembers, "I wanted enter the Army immediately, so that I could later on work on a ship, to see the world. But when I had the military doctors'

---

[12] *Praha* (Prague) was the capital of Czechoslovakia, which was in the throes of trying to break from Soviet rule.

examination and he measured my size, it was 158 cm and that would have been too small. So when he announced the size of 158 cm to the assistant, I corrected him: '160 cm.'"

Klaus didn't like the idea of being rejected by the military.

"The doctor told me to stand straight again and he measured. Again, he said '158 cm'

"I again corrected him: '160 cm.'

"Then he shouted to me: 'stand straight I told you!'. Again he measured and told his assistant: '158 cm.' Again I corrected him: '160 cm.'

"Then he smiled," Klaus remembers, "and said to me: 'I think you *really* want to enter the army.'

"I told him: 'Yes, Sir!'"

"So he told his assistant: write '160 cm', and I could finally enter the army as the smallest soldier. But to be the smallest, I was used to since Kindergarten, school and everywhere. This made me a kind of fighter."

Klaus was small of stature and could have avoided military service – but he wanted to serve in his nation's Armed Forces and notes that the experience was valuable to him.

"I stayed 9 months in the army and I was stationed in Salzburg." Klaus tell us. "When we had long marches, our Lieutenant (only a little bit taller then me) was very happy, when we were never complaining and walking till the end ... even when the big guys had to stop because they could not continue. So after 8 weeks training, we were supposed to get to certain units, like tank gunner, driver, kitchen, casino, etc. For me it was sure that I come to the kitchen or the casino, serving the officers. But on the day of selection, every soldier of our 140 person unit got his position. When it came to the kitchen staff, I thought, this is my turn."

"But my name was not mentioned." He went on. "So I was more happy, because casino was a fine job. But also here my name was not mentioned. We were only 8 men left. And here came the big surprise: 'You 8 men have to start from next Monday a special training of 2 weeks, which is very hard, but then you will serve as trainers'."

"Oh boy, this was a shock for me! Our Lieutenant was the rest of my time in the army very happy with my work. and also the young soldiers respected me and were happy, to be in my group. So later on that was the reason, why I spent several of my ship's vacation from to be again for 2 weeks again in the army."

He liked the Army.

"I was a boy scout and I loved the nature already in my childhood and sleeping in a tent, holding the night watch. Sitting around the fire in the evening was the beginning of my dream to see many countries and their natures.

"I was trained on pistol, machine pistol, automatic rifle, machine gun, heavy machine gun and tank cannon. We used the American tanks M41 and M42, which were left in Austria, when the United States Army left Austria in 1955."

Dona served in the Austrian Army at a critical time in history. His nation was in the process of reclaiming, reconstructing and updating its national identity – this time on a peaceful, self-governing constitutional foundation. It was a powerful national march, out of the chaos and confusion of the recent past with its overlays of failures, conflicts, defeat and occupation, onto the world stage as a rightful and righteous nation. Yet with every step of that march into the future, there was a swell of pride that embraced the past as well.

Klaus Dona, on duty with the Austrian Army.

The long history of the Austro-Hungarian Empire was worthy of remembrance and respect, and he was marching in the footsteps honorable warriors who served their empire in life – and all too often, in death as well.

What did Klaus and his comrades think about on those long marches that lengthened their strides and toughened their bodies? How did they pull themselves out of a keen awareness of aching feet and sore muscles, by choosing something more rewarding to focus on?

Girls, of course.

A cold beer and a card game in the Day Room tonight; watching a soccer match on TV.

Home. Wonder what my family's doing right now, at home?

When will I get a weekend pass?

Maybe just the luxuries of a hot shower to wash off the dust of the day, and a clean bed to fall into for a night's deep sleep ... versions of the things all soldiers think about, in all the armies of the world, past and present.

In all the wars, good and bad.

In his tour of military duty, Klaus proved to be an able leader and quite a marksman!

With all the weapons of all the ages, from sticks and stones to computer-targeting and modern nuclear weapons.

In the Schatzkammer (treasure chamber) of the Habsburg House museum in Vienna, the glorious military past of the Austro-Hungarian Empire is on well-guarded display behind glass, represented in an array of swords and uniforms, ceremonial robes, insignia and flags, among the other national treasures resting there.

There are artifacts from Rome and elsewhere in the Vienna Museum, Military Historical Museum and other museums in the region. and further evidence of glorious history in the statues and other monuments that grace the stately principal cities of the old Empire.

Those who believe in reincarnation might pause and wonder: was I there, at those historic battles? Did I help to defend Vienna from the Turks? Or did I slog my way through cold mud in World War I at the battles of the Isonzo? Such speculations were far from his thoughts at the time, but by serving in his nation's forces he had stepped into its tradition of military history. And history appealed to him.

CHAPTER 6

A WORLD OF OPPORTUNITY

What a delight it was for Klaus to visit the Acropolis in person!
It was a wonderful time to be alive.

It wasn't a perfect world in the late 1980s and early 90s –
it never is. Still, the wounds of World War II and the Cold War
that followed weren't quite so fresh in everyone's mind as they
had been only a few short years before. In spite of international
tensions and dividing lines, Europe was clearly on the mend.
Austria still held its traditional stance as a crossover nation
between Western Europe and the East, and was successfully
bridging past and present as well, with a vigorous rebuilding
program.

For an adventurous, intelligent young man like Klaus, the
world was an open door. He was a hard worker, and there were
jobs to be had. Where would he go? What would he see? *Life*
lay ahead of him, just crying out for him to latch onto it.

How would he approach it, and set himself on a track of
independence and exploration?

He traveled by train to London, were he wanted to work in an international hotel. But on the ship cruise from Le Calais to Folkestone he was checked by the British custom officers and after being questioned in Folkestone , because he did not have a working permit for England, he was sent that night with the same ship back to Calais. As he never gave up something easy, he took a train to Paris were he worked 6 month in a German Restaurant as a cook and than another 6 month at the famous Hotel Ritz as a Commis de Restaurant, were he served famous persons like Coco Chanel and many others.

After one year in Paris he returned to his home base and soon entered into the service of the Austrian army. There he spent 9 months serving as a tank soldier and also as a trainer for young soldiers, after which he and a friend of his went by car Tyrol to Hamburg and he started to work on a German ship.

Klaus and his friend were on the high road to adventure! It wasn't that difficult, actually. Pulling on a T-shirt and a pair of dungarees, he stepped into a pair of deck shoes, tucked his culinary skills into a handy duffel bag along with a few personal necessities, and signed on as a steward on a cargo vessel bound for ... where? ... Did it matter *where*? Not really. There was a whole *world* of seas to sail and ports of call to visit, out there waiting for him.

There's a certain cachet that comes with being able to say that you've "been everywhere, and done everything", and Klaus was quick to earn it. But his journeys weren't just about being able to *say* he'd been to Piraeus or Liverpool, Singapore or Tokyo. He wasn't just a passerby at remote geographical locales, collecting names like Buenaventura and Halifax, Hong Kong and Hamburg, Nahodka and Trieste and Suez, that he could drop into casual conversations later on, to impress a pretty girl.

It's not just the scenery that makes faraway places so fascinating – it's getting a bird's eye view of how other people live; learning their languages and being exposed to their customs. He took shore leave when it was to be had, and spent time immersed in those faraway cultures, every chance he got.

The timing of Klaus's voyages was significant, also. He was poised on a moment of 'living in the present' that stood on a slender bridge between past and future. When he first went to sea, air travel was just beginning to be affordable for ordinary people of modest means -- and modern advances in the telecommunications industry had yet to play their commanding roles in making it truly a "small world" for most of today's global population.

In his day, an adventurous young fellow could still 'go to sea, and see the world' in a tradition not all that far removed from the days of brigs and barks and whalers; of clipper ships and tramp steamers and the great floating-palace passenger liners that still dominated transoceanic luxury travel in his time.

The world was definitely there to be seen! Klaus fondly remembers his first sight of the Acropolis in Athens and other historical sites in Greece, and Carthage's ruins in Libya. He also ventured on short trips to the Sahara desert, to Jerusalem, to other historical places in Israel and to many other historical places in our multi-cultural world.

In December of 1970 he intended to spend two weeks in Colombia but met a beautiful girl there and ended up spending six months. During that time he traveled through Colombia, visiting places like Santa Marta, Popayan, and Medellin.

He also went back home to Austria from time to time.

"From 1971 – 1972 I made a 1 year private business school attendance in Innsbruck (Tirol)," Klaus reports as he speaks of his years at sea., "so that I could work on the next ship as chief steward and purser." I also had ten days vacation for every month worked aboard ship, but that was too long for me to sit around not doing anything , so I spent several times two weeks in the army for further training and exercise."

Back at sea once more, there was the profound experience of being out of sight of land for days at a time, feeling very tiny in a world of endless sea and sky.

We are both dwarfed by infinity, and embraced by it. There is a timelessness about it.

For an inquiring mind with a sense of history, it can bring visions of the distant past, before air travel existed in its present form, and when travel on land could be equally hazardous, with no roads or trails to follow ... for that part of Earth's history when watercraft, large and small, were the mainstays of human travel over long distances.

How long would it take to sail from Europe to North America, or from China to Colombia? It was certainly more than a hop, skip and a jump to Columbus! Nor was Thor Heyerdahl's more modern voyage on the Kon-Tiki an easy one, as he re-created the conditions of ancient journeys on a balsa raft! And how many adventurous folk set out and never saw dry land again, having been lost at sea?

Klaus managed to take a sightseeing sidetrip to the pyramids, while traveling in Egypt.

This ultra-ancient image, carved in stone, shows a ship with sails, rudder, figurehead prow, and oars ... with surrounding sea and sun overhead clearly represented.

There are ships of various sorts depicted in the pictorial records of the pyramids and on other ancient artifacts. Did the widely-scattered "mythical" civilizations of the distant past of the world have contact with each other, in those forgotten days of which we know little or nothing?

Was there in fact a global civilization on this planet, in ultra-ancient times?

Without evidence, we can only speculate. Yet as Klaus came to learn on his own journeys and by further research, there *is* evidence to that effect. Clearly, the numerous Out-of-Place Artifacts that he seeks out and displays, today, indicate cross-cultural contact between widely separated ancient civilizations. Most of those interactions would necessarily have involved sea voyages, presumably by those who created and maintained a series of international trade routes in pre-historic times -- far earlier than we would have thought possible. Yet here again, Dona's search for answers keeps uncovering more questions.

Based on the evidence shown in monuments, myths and artifacts, we have to consider that there may also have been air travel in those ancient times.

And what about space travel? Ah yes, there's a *big* question still in the process of being researched!

50

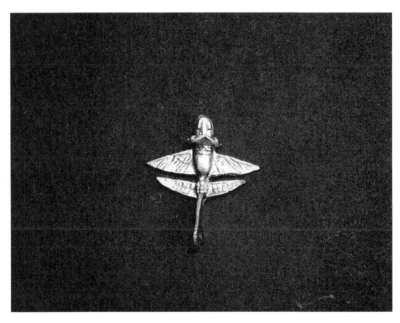

51

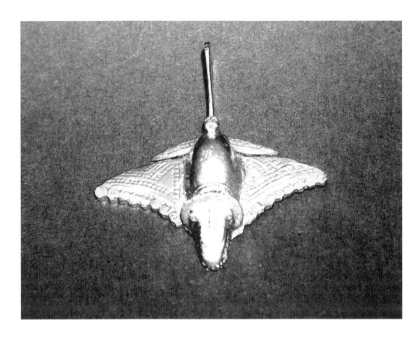

The golden artifacts pictured here were lent to the "Unsolved Mysteries Exhibit" by the holders of several collections, and were found by treasure-hunters in caches of the cultures of Calima, Tolima, Tairoina, in Colombia and at Diquis, Costa Rica. These and other similar pieces are sometimes identified by traditional scholars as representations of insect forms ... but they look more like airplanes and spacecraft to the less faint-hearted among us! Surely the cultures of the ultra-ancient world were more advanced and more diverse than we have (until now) presumed them to be.

This clean-lined artifact has often been called a bird. Does it look like a bird to you? Looks more like a plane to me.

Klaus Dona (center) travels widely in search of mysterious artifacts, crossing many international borders. Unlike the modern tomb raiders and pirates who seek treasure to sell it and enrich themselves, he works closely with local authorities to get their permission for his explorations – and to see that any treasures he may find are properly routed to the custody of the appropriate museums or departments of antiquities.

CHAPTER 7

PEOPLE ARE PEOPLE

Professor Jamie Gutierrez of Colombia, Dr, Vera
Hammer of the National Historical Museum in Vienna, and Klaus
Dona examining the "Genetic Disk" from Colombia.
The disc is made of Lydite.

It wasn't long before Klaus found himself serving in a series of new roles.

Well before his 30th birthday, he had indeed 'seen the world' and been exposed to a wide range of cultures. He's an open and adaptable fellow, and everywhere he went, he seemed to have a knack for fitting in. Differing cultures didn't faze him. After all, people are still *people*, no matter where you go.

"After the army I started to work on ships", he reminds us. "Then in 1976 I stopped working on ships, because I got married. My wife was Japanese, and came with me to Austria.[13]

---

[13] Their marriage has since ended in divorce.

At that time I worked (until 1982) in hotels in Innsbruck as Concierge and manager."

"Then for five years I worked as marketing manager for Asia at the Vienna Tourist Board. In September 1987, I opened my own office and started with many cultural projects from Austria to Japan and from Japan in Austria, like CD-recordings with the famous Vienna Boys Choir, with famous Japanese stars, and classical concerts in Japan."

Klaus mounted his first independent cultural exhibition in 1992 with "The Glory of the House of Habsburg" and has since done over 22 exhibitions in Japan and four Japanese exhibitions in Vienna.

During his early travels, Klaus had acquired a healthy collection of simple "can do" language skills, and these continue to expand. They serve him well, in today's world of cultural exchanges and global market linkages.

While he was finishing his tour of military duty, and crisscrossing the planet on the decks of various ships, the world had continued to expand. There was a global economy – and a global community – in the making.

The Cold War was winding down, although some hot ones kept cropping up here and there. Humanity was still in conflict with itself over various disputes (real or imagined), but there were also those around the world actively working toward *connecting*. When folks find out how much they have in common, instead of always looking for differences to fight over, then peace becomes possible.

People like Klaus are an important part of that process, just by being who they are. They have the insight to see beyond the fluttering banners of cultural differences, and their inquisitive natures prompt them to step (carefully!) through the illusive boundaries of various national traditions.

When we have sloughed off the contrasting views and habits of various societies and lifestyles -- from the most primitive to the most advanced cutting edge of techno-global civilization – we come back to basic humanity. And to the bottom line: people are *people*, the world over. No matter what our nationalities and ethnic backgrounds, we are a mixed lot: there are wonderful people in every culture, terrible people in every culture ... and a lot of in-betweeners, doing the best we can with what we have to work with.

For much of the Earth's history, one of the big separating factors has been the very structure of "civilization" or "society" itself. Those who fall under the broad generalization of "ordinary people" are programmed for a distancing *awe* upon finding ourselves in the presence of those who wear the mantles of royalty, celebrity, great wealth or other distinctions.

How are we supposed to deal with it? What's the correct protocol? Or do we have the right combination of sensitivity, adaptability and confidence to write it ourselves, as we go along?

It is the one of the measures of a man, as Rudyard Kipling wrote,[14] "..to walk with kings, nor lose the common touch."

Klaus and his companion examine ancient statues, as if asking "what do you have to tell us?"

Klaus soon found himself 'walking with kings' during his tenure at the Vienna Tourist Board., and his easy way of connecting with people of all nations and all stations in life stood him in good stead. When he came into contact with members of the

---

[14] From the poem "If", by Rudyard Kipling.

royal family of Japan, he listened carefully to their requests, helped to prepare just the right events and programmes for them – and planted the seeds of a warm personal friendship that would endure across the oceans and across the years.

Klaus with Hawaiian shaman Haleaka, at Kona in 2009.

People are *people*, and he liked them! He wasn't over-awed by them, and they liked him too. No doubt he was a breath of fresh air in their world, where an excess of respectful protocol can diminish the spontaneity of life and become a kind of prison in and of itself.

His growing fluency in the Japanese language made him an asset for the Tourist Ministry, and gave him the tools for continuing to deepen his understanding of world culture. So many things that were new to him were simply 'normal' to his oriental guests, and by the same token some things he took largely for granted were new and strange to them.

In one instance, Klaus was called upon to organize a visit to a performance in the royal theater of Schoenbrunn Palace, in Vienna. His Japanese visitors wanted to enjoy Mozart's music in concert in that particular theater, having heard that the composer himself had once given a concert there on that very stage, for Marie Antoinette.[15]

During the course of their conversations, Klaus realized that the history of the Habsburg Empire, with its web of interconnection to the royal houses of Europe, was largely unknown in Japan.. That gave him the seeds of an idea that would come to fruition later on, when he organized and presented an exhibit of priceless treasures, The Glory of the House of Habsburg, in Japan.

He took it all in stride: people are people, the world over. At the same time, sometimes the diversity of the world in which we live made him wonder: How did we end up with so many different kinds of people, on this planet?

Where did we come from?

Where did life on Earth begin, and when?

What were the first Earthlings like?

In time, he would devote a significant portion of his career to the search for answers to those provocative questions.

And as he delved into the search for deeper answers, he would keep finding deeper questions.

Jose Maldonado and Klaus at the Museo de las Culturas Aborigines in Cuenca, Ecuador.

---

[15] Marie Antoinette, at that time the reigning Queen of France, was the daughter of the Habsburg Empress Maria Theresa of the Austro-Hungarian Empire, whose summer home was Schoenbrunn Palace – so she was presumably enjoying the courtesies and pleasures of musical entertainment on one of her rare trips "home".

This mask is from a recent find in Bolivia, and made of stone with inlaid eyes. It was found with other similar artifacts, several of which might have been sized for a giant!

This portrait of an unknown lady looks Egyptian – but it was found in Colombia.

CHAPTER 8

SEEING BEYOND THE OBVIOUS

Klaus stands with Adriano Forgione (an Italian publisher and researcher) and Dr. Walter Moser in front of a so-called "giant tomb" in Sardinia, Italy, in 2010.

In yesterday's schoolbooks of the Western world's history classrooms, there are usually chapters about "The Age of Exploration and Discovery". There has been so much intense *modern* history to take into account, that the explorative era gets little more than a passing mention, these days. Yet it was significant: a time in which the nations of Europe, under the leadership and patronage of their respective royal rulers, reached out by means of sailing ships and courageous sea captains, to explore the world beyond their own familiar shores.

It was a milestone on the path to globalization, set upon the maps that were then still in the process of being drawn by bold adventurers.

They were Columbus and Magellan and Hendrik Hudson, Captain Cook and Prince Henry the Navigator; Cortez and Pizzaro Ponce de Leon and Amerigo Vespucci and the rest. They were fortune hunters and empire builders, traders and entrepreneurs; adventurers and explorers of all stripes, establishing the sea routes and blazing the trails ashore for the colonists who would follow.

But that was old news. Pretty tame stuff for young Klaus. What about Lief Ericson and the Norse expansions? Where did the Finno-Ugrians and the Magyars come from? What about the Roman Empire and Alexander the Great, and ancient Egypt?

What about Piri Reis? Who made that map for him? Were there others as well, that have been lost to the ages – or are they, perhaps, waiting out there somewhere, yet to be found?

His interest kept moving from common knowledge to uncommon knowledge; from the known to the unknown; from history and pre-history to mystery itself.

As the course of his life took him from one far-flung place to another, he kept running across artifacts, monuments, and myths that reminded him of similar ones he had seen or heard of elsewhere. The acronym "OOPARTS"[16] kept cropping up in his reading and in his thoughts.

His tenure as Austria's Director of Tourism for Southeast Asia and his years of working so many times in Japan meant more traveling, and on his travels he kept finding more provocative monuments and artifacts. So many of them looked like they belonged somewhere else.

They fascinated him. He wanted to see more of these collected artifacts for himself. He wanted to know: are they real?

---

[16] Out Of Place ARTifactS

"In 1998 I had the idea of bringing many of the so-called OOPARTS to Vienna and show them to the public --but also to give the science the chance to check them and find out whether they are real or not. So many of them, I thought, would be a hoax" he confides, smiling. "And this was the beginning of my research on out of place artifacts . It was also the start of a lot of problems for me."

Why are so many artifacts found 'out of place', scattered around the world?

Where were they made, and how did they come to be in their present locations?

Those questions would stick with him.

He couldn't set them aside until he had some answers – or at least until he came to some *logical* speculative conclusions that felt right to him.

That quest for truth has become a part of his life's work, and continues to this day.

"On every continent, in every country of the world, there are sayings, myths, and legends."[17] Dona notes. "My quests to bring mysterious archaeological finds to light have brought me to the conclusion that in many cases, and perhaps in all instances, some truth lies buried in them."

"Let's take the legends of Lemuria, MU and Atlantis. " he continues. "In 1984, a Japanese diver from the island of Yonaguni (to the South of the Japanese island of Ryukyu) found an extraordinary giant undersea structure of stone, that was probably built by human hands. Prof. Masaaki Kimura, an underwater geologist, has since then undertaken many years of examination of these objects, along with many other finds that have been uncovered in the meantime. He states that about 10,000 to 12,000 years ago there must have been a long continent lying from the northernmost Sachalin Group almost all the way to Taiwan.

Some say these stone placements are the result of natural formation, but Klaus disagrees. The perfect cuts where the stones

---

[17] Quoted from TRUTH OR ILLUSION by Klaus Dona, ©Klaus Dona, 2010, as it appeared in die waage, April, 2010. Used by permission.

join together cannot be thought to be natural phenomena, nor can the precision of the stone circle.

"The idea that they are natural formations came because they are out of scale to human proportions," he notes. "The stone steps are much too high for a human to be able to negotiate them, so the people who first investigated it just decided that it has to be natural, not manufactured."

"They didn't stop to think it could have been made to fit the proportions of giants," he continued during his January 2010 lecture in Hawaii, "and there are legends of giants all over the world, even here in Hawaii ..."

There are also stone tunnels, a giant stone head that Prof. Kimura calls "Sphinx", and an enormous stone amphitheater, with rows of seats with stairs."

"Parts of this structure reminded me of an enormous block of granite with a weight of more than 350 kg., that was found along with more than 350 other artifacts in 1984 in a cave at La Mana, Ecuador, by a team of goldminers ..." he continued in his article for die waage.

Klaus hasn't found all the answers, yet. It's still a puzzle. But he seems to have the knack for putting the pieces of that puzzle together – and the stamina to keep working on it!

Here is a scale model of the underwater structures near Yonaguni, Japan.

*These underwater monuments were found near Yonaguni, Japan,
on the sea floor near Okinawa. They are part of a vast complex
of such structures, and from their dimensions appear to have
been scaled to the proportion of giants. We can see the
proportional scale by comparing the size of the divers in the
picture to the size of the features of the monuments.*

CHAPTER 9

AN EXPOSE

Klaus Dona at the speaker's platform in Barcelona at the 2009
European Exopolitics Summitt Conference, " Time for Truth".

    As our human lives are in the process of being lived, our
primary focus is on ourselves and our immediate surroundings.
That is as it should be. Yet so many people in our world today
are settled into that modality, and never lift their eyes – or their
thoughts—to something that stands above and beyond the
obvious.

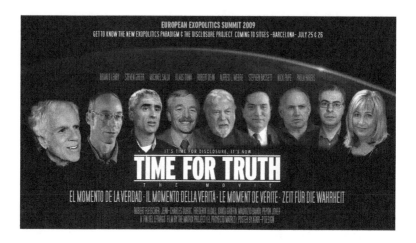

Klaus (fourth from left) is pictured among the "Time for Truth" program's featured speakers.

They move in an endless procession of days from today into tomorrow, and tend to lose sight of both the past – especially of the "yesterdays" that came before their personal experiences and memories kicked in., and are now relegated to "ancient history" – and the future. Others choose to extend their inner vision beyond the ends of their noses, if only because they feel that learning about the past can help us prepare for the future.

An inquiring mind isn't likely to be satisfied with the ordinary, repetitious detail of everyday life. From childhood, Klaus's natural curiosity had laid the foundations for a broader viewpoint. And delving into the mysteries of Earth's deep history is like eating peanuts: once you get started, you can't stop!

Once you start painting mental pictures on a broader canvas, even the little details of everyday life can be fascinating, in and of themselves. What are the parallels between societies and family life as it is lived today, and those of long ago? What are the differences? The commonalities?

What tools and implements did the ultra-ancients have to help them in their everyday lives? Once we start looking at the artifacts, we are often surprised to see how sophisticated and complex they are!

And what of the arts and sciences?

These ancient obstetrical tools (a knife and a "spoon", or forceps) were found near Bogota, Colombia. They are attributed to the Prae-Musica Culture, and date from about 500 B.C.

Judging from the monuments and artifacts that have survived the ages, we must assume that astronomy was more a part of daily life in the ancient times than it seems to be today. Were those cultures actually *more* advanced (in terms of their understanding of this planet's place in the Cosmos) than we are today? And if so, how can that be? There are archeological discoveries that make us wonder.

Sometimes it seems too much to grasp. "Impossible!" we exclaim to ourselves. And then we start looking for other explanations: for misinterpretations, unfounded assumptions and outright fraud.

There's a good market for ancient artifacts, in many parts of the world. And like any other market, it draws people who would like to take advantage of it. Clever artisans can use age-old patterns to make "old" Indian baskets to sell to the tourists in the American West, and modern knappers can chip out "Indian Arrowheads" by the bushel. If you question the authenticity of these items, the sellers will be quick to point out that if they were made by genuine Native American craftsmen, then they aren't "fake", but only "modern".

With a rising interest in collecting artifacts plus a string of new technologies (such as metal detectors and ground radar) to seek them out, new finds are constantly coming to light – and being offered for sale.

Apart from museums and other legitimate collectors, there are sure to be wannabe pirates for every treasure – and purveyors of fake goods, from knock-offs of expensive watches to copyright thieves preying on the intellectual rights of others, to producers of bogus antiquities.

So, are they *all* frauds, catering to the wishful-thinking and fantasies of a gullible public? No. That would be too easy!

Or, are *all* the intriguing artifacts genuine? No, of course not.

It's not that simple. You can't make a blanket determination. You have to examine every site and every find – and ultimately, every artifact – with a critical eye. You have to test and re-test – and even try to make a comparable copy of the item in question, to see if can be done ... and if so, *how* it can be done.

Klaus Dona was a dedicated skeptic.

A modern man in a modern world, he subscribed – as did the majority of his fellow men – to the principle of "impossibility", in which some extravagant claims just *had to be* frauds, because they were too wild and fanciful to be true. He felt no need to stray into the world of unfounded speculations and imaginative untruths; the "real" world of provable facts and replicable results would do nicely for him, thank you.

Deception made him uncomfortable – especially when someone was doing it blatantly, to turn a quick profit.

He got the idea of researching and presenting an exhibit on fake artifacts and fraudulent claims to historical authenticity: an expose□. Now, *that* would be an interesting exhibit!

He began putting a plan together in which various artifacts would be subjected to rigorous scientific examination by panels of experts ... who would presumably pull off the flimsy illusions, lay bare the truth, and prove them to be a series of imaginative hoaxes. He would start with some of the specific pieces that had attracted the most attention, including those often attributed to off-planet sources in popular modern New Age circles.

What tests could be brought to bear? He started making notes, and doing some research. Vienna was the perfect place for a project of that sort, with its credentialed and experienced cadre of scientific experts. They had the facilities and the equipment. They had the know-how.

He got in touch with the right people, and got the ball rolling. With testing in progress, he set about getting the necessary permissions to exhibit the artifacts in question, and roughed out the displays that would need to be built to house them.

Klaus and Dr. Vera Hammer of the National Museum in Vienna are shown here, testing some artifacts.

Then as the test results began to come in, Klaus was in for a surprise.

In the famed Crespi Collection[18], for example, only about 15% of the artifacts were fakes.

The others showed every sign of being genuine – and upon close and rigorous examination, they (further!) raised more questions than they answered. The same would prove true for items from diverse other sources as well, and before he knew it, Klaus's idea of doing an expose' exhibit had been shot out of the saddle ... along with his rigid skepticism.

As far as the idea of off-planet influence is concerned, the test had not been able to prove the concept to be false ... yet neither can it be proven, definitively, that the concept is *true*. Unless we have something clearly off-planet against which to compare them, we cannot "prove" that the creative technology behind these objects originated elsewhere, rather than on Earth.

But we have failed to prove that they did *not,* and it's hard to imagine that very early humans were as sophisticated as the artifacts indicate, on the basis of their own initiative and invention. It seems more likely that they had outside help from *somewhere.*

But where?
And when?
From whom?
And how?

---

[18] Father Crespi was a Roman Catholic priest, much beloved by his parishioners. Over the course of several decades, he amassed a collection of ancient artifacts brought to him by those in his congregation who knew he was interested in such things.

CHAPTER 10

CURIOUSER AND CURIOUSER

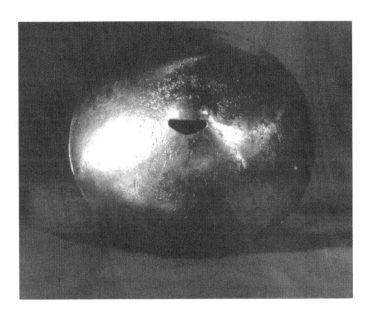

This round helmet made of metal was found in La Mana, Ecuador. It's meaning it unclear, although some esoterics think it may be original headgear pictured on some stones found nearby. The hole in the top of the helmet is thought to be an energy center that could activate energies in the astral body.

There came a point at which Klaus had to give up the idea of an Expose' exhibit. Its fate was sealed: another brilliant idea brutally murdered by a cold hard set of facts. His team of experts had identified some frauds, yes – but there weren't enough of them.

And too many items were definitely *not* fraudulent.

Now what?

The failure to expose them as fakes had not dampened Klaus's enthusiasm for researching ancient artifacts. On the contrary, it had only served to whet his appetite for more.

The ever-growing stream of questions kept circling around in his head. He kept finding more pieces to the puzzle and putting them into place, but was still a long way from being able to see the complete picture.

Were there people – and civilizations – on the Earth much earlier than we have traditionally believed? The archaeological evidence certainly points in that direction!

Where did they come from?

Was it from a single source, or from several different sources?

What were they like?

How could they have had astronomical knowledge? Why were their calendars so remarkably accurate?

How could they have had aerial-view maps? What about the Nazca lines?

What were their technologies?

Why are there pyramids all over the world, and how were they built? What role(s) did they play?

Did the several civilizations and societies interact with each other? The OOPARTS evidence indicates that they did.

They call it the "genetic disk", and it is one of the most interesting – and most confusing – finds of archaeology. It is made of black stone (lydite), and measures about 22 centimeters in diameter. The obverse and reverse sides are decorated with carvings and ornaments, separated by single vertical stripes.

One side shows biological details such as male sperm, female egg cells and the genitals, fertilized egg, foetus and a growing embryo. The other side shows scenes that could be interpreted as the cell division and depiction of frog-creatures in different stages.

The object has been examined in the Museum of Natural History, Vienna,m Austria, and has been assigned to the Musica culture. Those who have examined the stone include Dr. Vera M.F. Hammer, Dr. Aglund Eeboom, MD, Prof. Rudolf Distelberger, and others.

79

The scene carved on this stone has to do with an ancient legend in which powerful visitors from outer space are said to have come from Sirius/Orion to earth. The central figure holds a pyramid in his hands, and rays from his elaborate helmet seem to be depicted as flowing toward beings on the right who bow down before him.

CHAPTER 11

THE ROOTS OF MYTH

This figurine is called the "flying lizard", although it looks more like science fiction's Rodan than a pterodactyl. It was found in Acambaro, Guanajuata, Northwest of Mexico City.

Do you have a computer?

Is it hooked up to the internet?

If so, here's a little exercise you can easily do, to give you an idea of the prevalence and scope of some of Earth's major myths and mysteries.

When you enter "Atlantis" in the Google search box, you get about 36,000,000 results.

"Lemuria" will get you 91,000 and "Mu" racks up an amazing 265,000,000 results.

Of course, not every entry refers to these highly developed civilizations set on lost continents that are said to have sunk beneath the seas in the planet's distant past. Some are about hotels and casinos and NASA Space Shuttles; about Missouri University and shops and books and other products and all sorts of things. But clearly the *idea* of Atlantis and Lemuria (Mu) as lost civilizations/lost continents has survived the passage of innumerable ages, and is alive and well in modern public consciousness.

Whether people believe there's any truth behind these myths or not, they've heard of them. And among believers – and those who are curious, not knowing how much to believe -- the tantalizing search for the foundation of reality behind the myths goes on. Check out the available film documentaries and books on the subject, and you'll be overwhelmed by their numbers.

Klaus Dona, having been directly exposed to thousands of "out of place" artifacts that support the presumption that there were ultra-ancient civilizations *and that there was contact and trade between them,* is still looking for more answers. The possibilities are fascinating! He is among those engaged in researching these mysteries ... and on the track of drawing logical (and preferably verifiable!) conclusions as to the underlying myths of which the out of place artifacts are the remnant evidence.

Do all the OOPARTS point to directly to Atlantis or Lemuria, with specific links between the two? Well, no. Not *all* of them. Sometimes it seems like the evidence points in all directions, and suggests that it comes *from* every direction. And why not? If we are able to admit to ourselves that Atlantis and/or Lemuria may actually have existed, why not other ultra-ancient civilizations as well?

And why should we think that the depth of this planet's history has room for only *one* deluge, that affected the whole globe simultaneously and uniformly?

Could it not be that Atlantis and Lemuria are just the tips of the sunken-continent iceberg, when it comes to the sinkings (or other cataclysmic destructive events) of long ago?

There are so many mysteries. Dona's series of "Unsolved Mysteries" exhibits and lectures, which began in

2001, has brought a goodly number of them to the light of public attention. But *more* keep popping up, almost daily. Perhaps he has barely scratched the surface.

Certainly it is fair to say that in his search for answers, he has found a lot more questions!

How is it that ceramics from Japan & from Ecuador look so much alike that even world-renowned experts have trouble telling them apart? Or that ancient mummies found in the Atacama Desert of Chile, estimated to be between 6,000 and 9.000 years old, have the same DNA markers as the Ainu people of Japan?

When it comes to parallel myths and legends, we should also take into account that it's not just about pyramids and the remains of sunken cities. Nor is Klaus the first and only person to start tracking down the factual foundations behind the myths. Schliemann's search for Troy comes to mind, and on television today we can tune in to Simcha Jacobovici's "Naked Archaeologist" episodes, in which he tracks down (among other things) locations and details of Biblical history.

If you know Klaus Dona, you probably can't quite see him in a "Naked Archaeologist" role. Being in the TV-limelight in everyone's living room isn't his style. He's plainspoken and modest, rather than flamboyant, and is (as he's quick to tell you!) more comfortable sitting on a newly-excavated pile of dirt at a dig than standing behind a microphone or being videotaped by a camera crew. Beyond that, he's digging for something deeper and older than Ancient Greek cities or Bible lands. But like Schliemann and Jacobovici, he sifts through the myths and picks his locations carefully, before he visits the sites themselves to sift through the sands.

At this writing, he's following the folklore tales and trails of giants, hoping to unearth their bones for further study.

Among the remains of giants Klaus has examined so far are skeletons ranging from 2.6 to 7 meters tall, with skulls unlike those of homo sapiens. It appears that the oldest skeletons are those of the tallest individuals, and the overall size of this race diminished over a period of time. Their elongated skulls bear thicker bones than human skeletons, and are constructed differently: There is no fontanel at the crown, with three bony plates converging there. Instead, a single join-line runs right and left, across the top of the skull.

What species might these giants belong to? They are human-like, yes, but the differences are significant. DNA tests are now in the process of being made.

There are folk tales and myths about giants all over the world, and we find them recorded in the mythologies of a great many ethnic traditions including those of the Middle East, which is a hotbed of information on ancient civilizations. The Judeo-Christian Bible refers to a class of giants that came into being when the 'sons of heaven' looked upon the daughters of men, and found them fair and in a later account, mentions a giant Goliath by name. Sumerian myths from the same general region also speak of giant demi-gods[19] as hybrids of god/human origin[20], and note for the record one such later-generation individual named Og, who is said to have been a lot bigger than Goliath! And that's just for starters.

With so many myths and adventure tales of giants scattered widely across the planet, where do you even *start* to research them?

Fortunately, Klaus has some credible leads to follow. And he has probably already ruled out Pecos Bill, along with the flesh-eating cloud-dwelling fairytale giant of Jack and the Beanstalk fame, and America's giant lumberman Paul Bunyan ... to say nothing of his blue ox, Babe.

Of the numerous reptilian figures modeled in clay, this is one of the few that actually resembles what we would think of as a dinosaur.

---

[19]Nephilim
[20] see: "There Were Giants Upon the Earth", by Zecharieh Sitchin.

Prof. James J. Hurtak is shown standing in front of a giant human footprint in South Africa.

Klaus had an accident in a dangerous cave in the jungles of Ecuador, but managed to laugh about it.

*Curious artifacts on exhibit, so that everyone
might share their mystery.*

CHAPTER 12

THE TREASURE TROVE

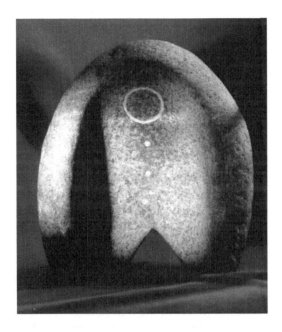

This stone features a hollow so big that a human head would fit perfectly into it. There are precious stones and a circle inlaid in the hollow at exactly the point where – according to Indian theories – the crown chakra is located. The crown chakra is said to be the energy-connecting point between an individual and his or her higher spiritual-energy resources.The Earth is full of treasures yet to be discovered. The evidence of civilizations that came and went before our own is layered, one era upon another, on – and beneath – the surfaces we walk upon or sail upon today.

Klaus Dona is a dedicated treasure-hunter who comes not to plunder or to pirate, but to rescue and recover, to restore, to study and *understand*. He and his like-minded companions are a new breed, whose desire for fame and fortune (if, indeed, there is to be any) takes a distant back seat to the quest for history and truth.

They aren't all dashing adventurers like Indiana Jones, and neither are they necessarily modern-day spiritually-motivated Sir Galahads on a high-minded quest for the Holy Grail. For some, the quest for history is enough, in an of itself.

Some of them are wealthy collectors who don't need more money, and would probably shy away from fame if attempts to visit them. They keep a low profile. Yet theirs, too, has long been a pivotal role in bringing the legacies of the distant past to collecting points, where they can be safeguarded and cared for. These legitimate explorers and researchers want to see the planet's most mysterious and most enduring treasures safely into the keeping of global preservationists – preferably within the regions in which they have been found -- where they will be respected rather than plundered.

All too often, one emerging culture has ridden roughshod over the remains of a previous one, heedless of the significance of what is being trampled underfoot. It's happening today, in the rainforests that are being destroyed for croplands by expanding populations, by industrialists (and governments!) who harvest natural resources for profit, and in the chaos of under-developed countries, unstable societies and failed nations. Can't we at least rescue *some* of the timeworn treasures, before it's too late?

Somehow, we feel it: the time is now.

The time for finding the records – and for sharing them with the world – has come.

Klaus's journeys of discovery lead not only to mountain caves and deepsea dives and desert digs, but also to the storage rooms and rows of shelves in private collections, stacked high with precious artifacts.

His plans for the next expedition, and the next and the next, are mapped out at least partly by the quality of the research material he has to work from. There's a lot of information available to a serious researcher. Once the right people know he's interested, they find their way to him.

Then when he finds himself holding a basket of diverse clues in his hands, he must sift through them and consider the practical aspects: what country is the find said to be in? Will the government cooperate, and give permission for an expedition to go there? Sometimes, you even have to ask yourself if the government itself can be trusted. If you make a valuable find and report it to them in good faith, will they also act in good faith to safeguard it – or will corrupt officials at various levels sell it and keep the money?

Who owns the land you want to dig on? Will they give you permission, and be willing to make some fair agreement for the proceeds of the find, when something valuable is found?

In a recent television news report, we learned of a treasure-hunter hobbyist with a metal detector who had the feeling that a British farmer's field might have something interesting on it – and it did, mostly in the form of golden artifacts resting near the surface. From the way they were scattered over a wide area, one might conclude that they had been dropped by fleeing plunderers trying to escape, as they were driven out by a more powerful military force.

When?

Who?

How?

The antiquarians are in the process of researching that now.

The treasures themselves went to the British Museum, and the finder and the farmer, having come to an agreement before the search was undertaken, ended up splitting a hefty fortune, 50-50.

If you're tracking down an underground cache, how easy (or how difficult!) is the access to it?

If it's a private collection situation in which the artifacts have already been recovered and assembled, will the owners give permission to allow them to be seen, studied and photographed? Would they be willing to lend some selections from among their treasures, to be placed on exhibit?

If it's a sacred site guarded by the locals and their shaman (as is often the case), will they agree to help you or will they try to stop you? How can you win their trust? Klaus has been fortunate in that regard: most of the shamans, if they are genuine, are smart enough – or intuitive enough – to see that he is going to respect their traditions and can be trusted. If there are ceremonies to be observed, he will be willing to participate. He doesn't necessarily have to adopt their beliefs; he just has to be courteous.[21]

If you're approached by a local fellow who has something he says he dug up in his field that he wants to sell, is it real? Sometimes he offers it so cheaply that it's worth buying, taking a chance that it can be authenticated. Is it stolen? What about the laws of his country? Do they permit the sale of artifacts that are unearthed on private property? Some do, and some don't.

And of course, the big question: does he have any more things like that back on the farm, for you to have a look at?

A lot of planning goes into an expedition – and Klaus stays busy doing his homework, checking out the details. It's expensive, too – and that's before you even get to the point of having the researchers authenticate everything, to say nothing of working with a museum toward mounting an exhibit! The fee you pay to see an exhibit will most likely be used to fund the next expedition, and the next exhibit.

He laughs about not being "Indiana Dona", brandishing a bullwhip and dodging Nazi villains on their Fuehrer-driven search for magical power objects. Neither is he obsessed with finding evidence of ancient prophecies that will reveal (or confirm) the exact date at which we may expect the end of the world to come crashing down on us. Nevertheless, the hunt for OOPARTS is exciting – and demanding.

The quest for ancient artifacts is not for the faint-hearted, the fragile or the lazy ... but if your cup of tea it can be wonderfully rewarding.

---

[21] as long as their traditions don't include a serving of "long pig". He's not that courteous.

*Examining an artifact, Klaus wears his special glasses
to help determine whether it is genuine or not.*

*This octagonal stone plate, found at La Mana, Ecuador, is inlaid
with seven concentric circles. Some have interpreted it to be a
mandala, with the inlays representing the seven major chakras.*

This beautifully-polished stone represents the head of a snake, with inlaid eyes of silver. It was found in Ecuador.

Klaus is shown here with his friend Frank Pryor, checking out an artifact – but this one turned out to be a fake.

CHAPTER 13

THE MYSTICAL MOTIF

It's not an easy task.

Bridging the gap between myth and history takes meticulous research, logical inferences, good instincts, and a generous sprinkling of lucky guesses. When it comes to clues, you work with what you have ... and feel your way along.

Klaus Dona is a practical person. He wants the OOPARTS exhibits and related work to be as scientifically grounded as possible, but he comes at it from a broad perspective. If he rejects clues that come from mysterious and the mystical origins out of hand, before the project even gets started, he's going to be working within some narrow limits ... so there are times when he chooses to 'go with the flow' and see where it takes him. The critical evaluations can come later, when he has something concrete to work with.

At the same time, Dona must also take a broad view of what the OOPARTS research yields, even though that means setting aside "conventional wisdom" in the process. Otherwise, his work would add little or nothing to our understanding of ultra-ancient planetary history, but would be a simple re-hash of old data, old interpretations, and old opinions (right or wrong!).

If you're going to break new trails, you can't just keep following the old pathways others have mapped out.

The OOPARTS category is especially challenging, because of how far back we have to look for the surviving mythologies they relate to. Sifting through the myths themselves to slough off the fantasy-and-fluff overlays is a good first step, yes, but we cannot reject *all* mythologies and mystical interpretations out of hand, without research and consideration. Some of the most startling insights and conclusions may actually prove to be the most accurate, when all is said and done.

Beginning with the artifacts themselves, fitting the pieces of the puzzle together as best we can, we come up with (so far!) clear evidence that points to the existence of several ultra-ancient civilizations that were interconnected by trade and travel. These various civilizations are by no means all alike – there are differences among them – yet there are commonalities, as well.

In virtually every instance, we are confronted by the fact that the ultra-ancient civilizations were <u>much older</u> than has been previously supposed, and (in many cases) <u>more advanced</u> than those that followed after them.

How does Klaus respond to that, and what explanation does he give?

"It's still a great mystery to us," he notes, to sum it up. "We still have so many questions that have not yet been answered. We are putting the pieces of the puzzle of life on Earth together, but we don't have all the pieces yet ... so we only get to see part of the picture and keep adding to it, a little at a time."

"After so much time and so much research," he continues, "we still don't know how the pyramids were built. We have some ideas about it; we can speculate, but we don't *know*."

"How were the stone henges built, and how was it calculated that they should be placed precisely where they are located, to correlate features of this planet with stellar constellations?" He goes on to ask. "How did they know about astronomy in those times, to make calendars?"

"And what about the other sciences? Among the artifacts there are some very precise surgical and obstetrical instruments that the medical experts tell us are as good or better than anything similar we have today. And how were they made? We don't know."

"There are so many mysteries," Klaus reminds us. "What about the maps, that show what can only be described as aerial views of parts of the planet? And the Nazca lines"

"Everything of this kind points to an ultra-ancient global civilization that had technologies – including air travel – millions of years ago, that have for the most part been lost to modern memory", he emphasizes. "It sounds quite impossible. Yet when we look to the artifacts, and to the remnant mythologies of various cultures plus ancient historic references such as Biblical, Veddic, Sumerian, Akkadian histories[22], the evidence is there.

"Where did these technologies and their civilizations come from?" Klaus asks. "Did they evolve here on Earth over a

---

[22] The works of Zechariah Sitchen are full of detail on these.

long period of time, only to de-evolve and fall into pre-memory when the time of their cultural ascendancy and dominance was over?"

We don't have the answers.

"...but to me," Dona asserts, "that seems very unlikely. It is even harder to believe than the idea that this planet was in contact with other people from outside the Earth – space visitors and even space colonists, if you want to think of them that way."

If there were space visitors and space colonists on Earth in ultra-ancient times, where are they now? What happened to them?

Most people who ponder these particular mysteries will tell you: they're still here, within ourselves. *We* are their descendants, who have carried the crucial threads of their highly advanced intellectual and creative qualities through a long evolutionary process of intermingling with indigenous Earth folk.

Zechariah Sitchen postulates that off-planet genes, handed down from the ultra-ancient 'gods and goddesses' through a series of 'demi-gods and demi-goddesses', are responsibile for the 'DNA and mitrochondrial DNA differences (223 of them!) that upgraded us from wild hominids to Modern man', hundreds of thousands of years ago.[23]

To put it into Native American spiritual context, we are the children of both Father Sky (the star-colonists) and Mother Earth (the planetary evolutionary process through which early humanity developed).

He has heard the myths, the mystical explanations, and the speculations. What does Klaus Dona think of all this?

"I don't know" he admits, truthfully. Indeed, *nobody* can know for sure.

"It's still a mystery, " he continues, "Surely it is true that 'the Lord works in mysterious ways'. We can see the hand of the ultimate Creator in all these mysteries, but we do not know the grand plan behind it all. "

"I want to keep looking for more pieces of the puzzle, that we can keep fitting them together" he confides in a personal aside. "And I want to keep bringing the OOPARTS – the evidence – into the light of discovery and exhibition, where

---

[23] Quoted from "There Were Giants Upon the Earth" by Zechariah Sitchen, Bear & Company, 2010.

everyone can have a look. Where everyone can decide, each one for himself and herself, what to think of it."

And what happened to those early civilizations?

"Oh, that's easy!" Klaus reminds us. "They were destroyed by floods and earthquakes, all kinds of earthchanges and calamities, all the disasters of the ultra-ancient times that we have heard about – and the ones we haven't even heard about, also! -- Atlantis and Lemuria and all the rest of them. There are so many pieces of them that are still buried in the Earth, or swallowed by the sea. And of course they are also destroyed by time itself, until and unless we go looking, and find what's left of them."

"... finding them and trying to understand them," he muses. "that's the fun part!"

We can see that he means it.

He has found a job that's *fun!*

This grouping of a black stone goblet and 12 small matching cups was found in a gold mine in La Mana, Ecuador. They are inlaid with "points" that have been identified as star constellations of Orion, Sirius, and the Pleiades. The inside of the cups show a red stone point inlay at the center.

*This discus from Phaistos is a replica from the archaeological
museum, Iraklion. Found in Crete, it is made of clay and features
incised Cretan heiroglyphics whose development dates to about
2,000 B.C.. So far, it has not been deciphered – even with the aid
of computers. Prof. Cyrus H. Gordon of Brandeis University
notes that there may be some parallel between
Minoic script and Mayan script.*

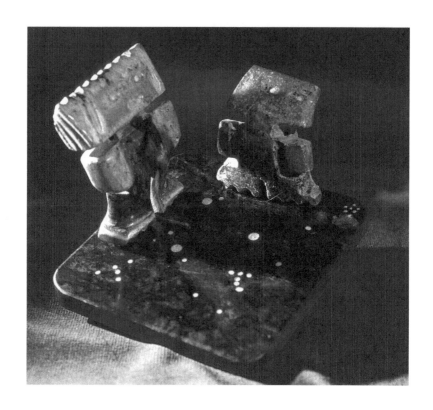

Two broad-faced figures are fixed on this polished black stone plate, their heads raised as though looking at the sky. It was found in La Mana, Ecuador, and features inlays showing different star constellations.

CHAPTER 14

THE KEEPERS OF THE FLAME

*The seekers of truth: (from left) Andreas Kalcker, Jordan
Maxwell, Bill Ryan of Project Avalon,
Marcel Messing, and Klaus Dona.*

They are the shamans and historians, the tribal elders and
the archivists, the private collectors and the museum curators, the
storytellers and researchers, the archaeologists and
paleontologists, geologists and investigative researchers, the
mythmakers and the myth-debunkers; the investigative reporters
and the feature writers; the artists ... the seekers. They are the
keepers of the flame, who gather the memories of the past and

keep them alive. Their stock in trade is an insightful knowledge of some aspect of the *truth* of our planetary home.

If they are looking for "the simple truth", they're out of luck. The truth is anything but simple.

The truth – the *whole* truth – is beyond human understanding. We can't possibly see all of it at once. It is too vast and varied. Instead we see a series of *reflections of facets of the truth*, as one might see reflections from the facets of a revolving mirrored ball on the dance-floor, shining as the light plays across it. Its rainbowed reflections are cast broadly for all to see; inviting impressions and interpretations.

When we look at the artifacts of our planet's historic, pre-historic and ultra-ancient past – and especially the OOPARTS, that don't fit easily into the categories of our preconceived notions of conventional thinking – we are confronted by the reflections of bits and pieces of the truth that may well be new to us. Putting it all into a perspective that "fits" for us can be a challenging task. There's so much opportunity for interpretive speculation – which may or may not be helpful or insightful.

Klaus Dona sticks as close as he can to the reflections of truth – the *hard evidence* – and leaves the interpretation to others.

"The artifacts speak for themselves," he says. "We can learn as much as they have to tell us – and then the rest is still a mystery."

If you ask his opinion, he will tell you what he thinks, based on the evidence – but he will not say "this is a certainty."

Nothing is certain.

He is still digging for answers ... and finding more questions.

The keepers of the flame are quick to see that he is one of them: he will do his best to be true to the historical evidence that comes before him, and he will be sensitive to the traditions, beliefs and opinions of others with whom he comes in contact along the way. Often they see something in him that gives them confidence, and are willing to share their knowledge – and the secrets of their local artifact caches – with him.

There's something about him that makes them say to themselves *...here is the right person to whom I can show my treasure ... here is the right person to whom I can tell my story.* And so often, also, *I know someone who would like to connect with him.*

A natural information-sharing network just seems to happen around him in a free-flowing way. Key people cross his path, and their skills and knowledge connect with his grid and his team. The right information pops up at the right time, and is added to the databank of his collections.

What's behind it?

Luck? Coincidence? Divine providence? It doesn't matter.

Warnings from the locals, about snakes and spiders, rockfalls and unstable terrains (to say nothing of bandits or drug cartels in the area!)? He will be on his guard, or pass one site by for a less dangerous one.

Evil spirits, guarding the treasure? Well, maybe they aren't really *evil* spirits. Maybe they are just guardians of the treasure, and if the local shaman greets them correctly (or tells Klaus how to greet them correctly), they will see that this is the right time – and the right team – for the treasure to be revealed. He does not laugh at these warnings, or dismiss them as superstitious.

"That is not necessary," he tells us. "It is better to show respect for the local beliefs and stories, we can get along much better that way."

"...everybody has their own way of thinking, and their own way of doing things," he adds in afterthought. "You don't have to agree with their beliefs; you just have to be willing to listen and approach it from their way."

Klaus is good about that, even if he feels silly doing it.

"You have a very strong past-life connection to Quetzecoatl," a mystic once told him, knowing he was going to be working in an area where the Feathered Serpent traditions and energies were prevalent. "You must stand before his statue, and say 'here I am! Your right-hand man is back!'. Then he will help you find what you seek."

When the time came, he remembered those instructions ... but standing before the great stone Quetzecoatl image, he felt a bit self-conscious and (although he was alone) didn't want to be overheard, speaking to a statue. Still, he did it anyway.

"Here I am. Your right-hand man is back." He mumbled it under his breath.

Immediately, a local man approached him and introduced himself. By then, Klaus was not entirely surprised to discover that the fellow was a shaman as well as a knowledgeable source of much information.

The next time he found himself in a similar situation, directing key phrases to a stone statue or an unseen spirit, he was a lot less self-conscious about it!

"I'm glad for all the help I can get!", Dona says.
He doesn't have to examine it super-critically; he just lets it flow ... and that seems to be working very well for him.

The keepers of the flame are quick to sense that he is one of them, and are drawn together by natural affinity.

This un-retouched photograph of Klaus in a nuragh was taken on a recent dig in Sardinia. There was no light source to explain either the white light at heart level or the blue light above his head. What does it mean? "I don't know," Dona responds.

*Here Klaus is seen with his very good friend
and helper, Dr, Walter Moser.*

*When this picture was taken, Klaus had just finished his research
of a big tunnel system in Sardinia.*

Klaus stands beside a giant phallic symbol in
Villa de Leyva, Colombia.

*Klaus is shown here with
his good friend Dr. Jaime Gutierrez.*

*Klaus and his friend Dr. Jaime Gutierrez are shown together in
an underground tunnel in Colombia.*

*Klaus Dona and author Laurel Steinhice
at a conference in Hawaii in 2009.*

*The famous Austrian professor Ernst Fuchs, shown here with
Reinhard Habeck and Klaus Dona, visited the "Unsolved
Mysteries" Exhibition in Vienna in 2001.*

CHAPTER 15

WHAT'S NEXT?

One size does <u>not</u> fit all.

From the abundant evidence of artifacts recovered and carefully studied over the past few decades, we must logically conclude that *sentient "human" life on this planet is much older than had been previously thought or believed.*

We are using the term "human" loosely, because from that same evidence, we must also conclude that *the "people" who lived here millions of years ago were not all alike.*

Some were gigantic, to varying degrees.

Some were tiny, by comparison to modern human norms.

Some had physical features that were not "human", by definition.

Some recent Southeast Asian finds are beings dubbed "hobbits"[24] in the press, based on their small stature and reflecting the fact that samples of their DNA have classified them as other than human. Are they a line of hominids that evolved on this planet and then died out? We may well suppose this to be the case – but we don't actually *know*. It is another question without a clear answer.

Klaus Dona has by no means maxed out his interest in the mysteries of our planet's history, and for the focus of his next exploration he has cast his eyes on the remains of the ultra-ancient people themselves.

There are the bones of giants in the OOPARTS collections he has studied thus far – and the remains of tiny humanoid creatures as well. According to the anomalies they present, one can't definitively classify them as truly *human* ... yet they are obviously not just animals, either. They are *people*, somehow, and we know very little about these people. Klaus hopes to learn more.

Turning to the data he has already gathered and to the network of contacts he has put together, he has several leads on where to go looking for more ultra-ancient bones, and is in the process of getting the necessary permissions for a series of new digs. Whatever he comes up with will be carefully examined on its way to the appropriate museum.

There are countless treasures yet to be brought to light, and the hunt is by no means over!

While there is always the possibility – and even the hope!-- that some discovery may bring fame and fortune along the way, it would be unfair to say that Klaus is in it for the money. His passion is for the adventure, itself, and for the satisfaction of seeing lost treasures restored to a place of honor and respect, each in the history and context of its own country and culture.

There is a segment of our modern society in which interest in the history of ultra-ancient civilizations is still growing. We want to find more pieces of the puzzle, and are eager to keep trying to put them together.

Klaus Dona is one of our strongest resources in that quest, and we look forward to his bringing *more* ultra-ancient

---

[24] The term is borrowed from the popular fiction of J.R.R. Tolkien.

artifacts to light for us, in public exhibits and presentations to be shared with the world.

Indeed, he intends to keep digging for answers ... knowing that he will also keep finding more questions, along the way.

In the Spring of 2001, Klaus Dona (left) and Reinhard Habeck (center) visited with Professor Cabrera at the Ica-Stones Museum in Ica, Peru.

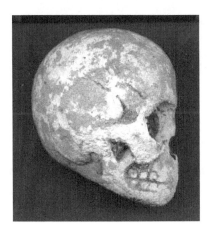

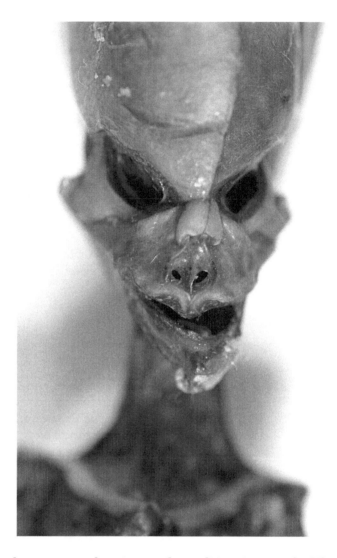

Are there more explorations and expeditions in store for Klaus Dona? He certainly hopes so! He is particularly interested in tracking down information on humanoid remains and lore, with an eye for evidence of giants, little people and other anomalous folk, such as those whose bones are shown here.

AFTERWORD

When I first began channeling Edgar Cayce (in June, 1988), I was told that information leading to the recovery of the lost records of Atlantis and Lemuria (also known as Mu) would becoming to the surface, and that I would have a part in it. I believe that's what's happening, now.

Those who are involved in the kind of exploration and research that leads to the discovery of OOPARTS – among them Klaus Dona – are tracking down the "lost records" and bringing them to light.

The whole process fascinates me!

I haven't tried to tell the story of the OOPARTS themselves – there are far too many of them, and I leave that to Klaus. Rather, I hope to introduce him and his work to a broader band of public attention, particularly within the English-speaking world. (Herr Dona's own written works are available in German, but few have been translated into English, as yet. His filmed interviews appear in several languages on DVDs and internet presentations, and his "Unexplained Mysteries" exhibits and lectures are presented internationally.)

Interest in this explorative focus is growing, in the mainstream societies of many nations. Everywhere you turn on the Educational TV channels, in bookstores and on the internet, you run into something that's related to the study of ultra-ancient Earth history – and to the implications these studies and focal points may have on Earth's future!

I've learned so much, during the preparation of this book! Yet like Klaus himself, as he digs for answers, I keep finding more questions.

There's more to OOPARTS research than a mere handful of explorers, researchers and exhibiters can handle. It would take an *army* of researchers to do it justice! So I ask myself, who will be the adventurous searchers, archivists, preservationists, and academicians of the future, hot on the trail (as Klaus is now!) of relics of ultra-ancient planetary history? Who will keep finding new pieces of the puzzle, and fitting them together?

Who will *care* enough to keep searching for artifacts ... and for insight and understanding?

Maybe some of the young people who come to Dona's "Earth's Mysteries" exhibits will be bitten by the love-of-OOPARTS-adventure bug, and become intrigued by the questions they raise.

Maybe they, too, will start digging for answers.

I hope so, because I am sure there are still a great many "lost records" out there, waiting to be found.

Laurel Steinhice
Nashville, Tennessee, 2011

RECOMMENDED RESOURCES

Unsolved Mysteries Vienna exhibition catalogue, written with Reinhard Habeck

Im Labyrinth des Unerklärlichen, written with Reinhard Habeck

Im Zeichen der Pyramide, written with Karl Schmeisser
DVD -

ABOUT THE AUTHOR

Laurel Steinhice is a woman of many interests and many talents. She is the founder of The LightSource Group and serves as voice and energy channel for a great many distinguished Spirit Guides, among them Edgar Cayce, Mother Mary, The Rainbow Angels (Archangels Michael, Rafael, Azreal and Gabriel), Ashtar, Nicola Tesla, Carl Sagan, Benjamin Franklin, Isa (the Christ) and the Buddha.

A Healing Minister of the Christian Churches of St. Thomas in America, she teaches self-healing classes and does individual self-healing counseling. She is also a Reiki Master, and a Life Member of the International Association of Counselors and Therapists.

Laurel is a member of American Mensa, as are all four of her adult children. A widow, she has three grandchildren and makes her home in Nashville, Tennessee.

You may contact Laurel at steinhice@earthlink.net or P.O. Box 50145, Nashville, TN 37205

BOOKS BY
LAUREL STEINHICE

(Metaphysical and General Interest)

The LightSource Group Imprint:

<u>Klaus Dona: Digging for Answers</u>

<u>Edgar Cayce's Self-Healing Tips</u>

<u>The Rainbow Angels' Guide to Color, Crystals and Healing</u>

<u>The Rainbow Angels' Guide to Exorcism</u>

<u>The Rainbow Angels' Guide to Earthchanges</u>

<u>The Rainbow Angels' Guide to Earth-Healing</u>

Also from The LightSource Group:

<u>Trees in God's Garden</u> by Lisa Hanes,
Laurel Steinhice, Channel

BOOKS BY LAUREL COLEMAN STEINHICE

(Historical Non-Fiction)

The Marion Group Imprint:

<u>Marion</u>

<u>Marion's Child</u>

<u>No Denial</u>
co-authored with Marion S. Coleman and Charles C. Steinhice

Books are available through Amazon.com or may be ordered through local bookstores.

For further information, see:
www.lightsourcegroup.com or www.laurelsteinhice.com

CPSIA information can be obtained at www.ICGtesting.com
Printed in the USA
LVOW01s0010160114

369527LV00009B/276/P

9 780983 000303